Emeralds and Charcoal

David Beersdorf

Published by: ILYNMW Publishing

www.ILYNMW.com

Copyright 2014 by David Beersdorf

david.beersdorf@gmail.com

Cover Design: David Beersdorf

Illustrations: David Beersdorf

ISBN 978-0-9913244-5-3

This book is dedicated to…..

Contents

Preface

I started writing this book when I was sitting in my World Literature class at Kennesaw State University fall semester of 2013. I wrote it in an attempt to express and work through pain and frustration in my life. I apologize if it's weird; I apologize if it's discouraging at times. Though it may not seem like it, this book (from beginning to end) tells a story, and I believe it should be read that way.

Nach Bhfuil sé seo Eolaíocht

I

Open up into the night
sky of all the times we
tried to kill many numbers
that never did exist.
Make a list of a
thesis: my life is a _____.
Green tape on an off-brown
carpet surrounded by the
tens of flies seemingly
eager to learn.
But the burn outside
the windowsill masks or
shines upon the true beauty
that comes from clasping Styrofoam.
Why would a dome be in such
plane view of this
marvelous catastrophe
provoking a plethora of
emotions, but mainly attraction?
Merely a fraction of slightly
smaller stones actually face
the front,
but if thine own would
face down they would see that
this is not science.

But the reliance in the compliance
                    of science is as frivolous a
                    foreshadow as leaving the long
                    way merely to glance and admire
                    the art of your skin.
          So where does one begin to
      imagine the upward motion
of daisies ceasing for all
          of eternity?
      When taciturnity, being the only
            prevention, leads to slightly less
            than an uprooted organ that one
                        is eager to let.
                  And before the realization of
            broken bet,
      the sun has set.

To Ponder

Think
Mind
To Wonder
Brain
All is vanity
Spit the sugar out
Leave the nails
Gums can bleed
Just for the felling
How can one keep warm alone?
Alone?
A lonesome, ominous, night excursion?
No

Why Do I Think?

"How are you sir?"
How am I?
How *am* I?
What am I?
I'm not yours
Please, don't touch my face
Unless you mean it
I know you don't
Do I enjoy being sad?
Yes

Zero

Once there was a man who used to smoke hares to the point that they were far too rare a creature to be considered worthy of a standing ovation from a tree. This idea of a man stood between the termite pile only to move forth into the wooded space that was previously unvisited by merely ideas. "Strive strive" was his anthem of the close distant that always seemed to get sick right before the hares would take the main stage of equals. Scales moved. It's even now, due to the opening of McNevin's shop. Only one hare he never ate, and decided to name him McGrevin. "This particular hare is now mine," he exclaimed as he trained McGrevin to smoke hares and nonentity. Ten.

Five

His favorite number is five, mainly because the nature of living qualified

him to study what is commonly known as ideals. McGrevin's training was

complete, but entirety of his morals had never been fully tainted. Forced

to exterminate his brother's favorite being,

no average individual could number the amount of ink spilled.

II

But on this day, what is
  traditionally known as "absences
   of sight" has now covered
    NO,
completely and wholly masked
      the alleged, miniature, transparent,
    frozen, pond purposely place
  perpendicular to the off-brown.
     Cups, now lifting down more often
       than empty coupons, resting
        emotionless upon newly dusted
        symbol of a meal.
          What does the (steal) average
          wretch of a "carnivore" have
           left to do but what society
         (ape-like) of his has now
        deemed normal as placing his
      cask upon newly shined symbol
    of assembly before the tens of
    rows of tempting leaves that
   guiltily excite that which has been
  born into wretched expectations: him?
  To break even one off the stem
of carnal-normism, would he
     knowingly ingest THE WORM; and

7

!THIS
my reviled answer, is the cause
nor/and result of a generation
who deems a breast as anything
less than that which has been
handcrafted by holiness:
art.
Who might imagine the start of an
environment so grotesque beginning with
such humane perfection in the
very same mind of Artist.
And still every detail pans out to
infinite supremacies in a far
more immaculate manner than if
by some flaw, fate itself
had been sloppily left in the hands of him:
the derelict.

Half Shut Eyes

The multiple views of perplexed certainty.

Awaken the eyes of the breathless.

Can hearts that have stopped beating begin on their own?

Open

Close

Open

Close

Open

Close

Side to side

Side to side

Left to back to right

Right to back to left

Eventual slumber

A short slumber

A scorpion interrupted slumber.

Constructing romanticized dreams upon rotten lumber

III

Coming down the eternally winding
  gravel thoroughfare, would I
    make the ever-present gaffe
    of perceiving the ferns
        to be humans as well.
Some spell had been cast, not only
          changing forever perspectives of sight,
      but moreover the sensation of
  touch would never be the same.
      What possible name could have come
    over mind, that while silking
      down inside of steel box
        and elastic poles penetrating out
          of unmasked pond, did *they*
            perceive the invisible motion of
              a dry nature to be none other
                  than her skin.
      The dew is not her exudation,
    so then why must the wind be
    her shawl?
  I was blind when I saw
  myself standing, but sitting
motionlessly moving, perpendicularly
evermore down and fantasizing
over knowledge that I feared
      I was to never possess.

Keats did address this knowledge,
           but why must he know and
           not I?
      Was his eye less cursory than
           that of mine?
      Never to feel the intertwined or
           the mystery of the warmth of
           machinery life?
                Oh the strife of longing and
purity covered hills and mountains,
   they rise and fall; and to feel
      with my own cheek their very
           life, not out of lustful desire,
           but simply to know.
                     Shall I ever know?

The Planet

O sweet air!
inhaled from the atmosphere of a planet unseen.
Only rumors of a future happening that
cannot come more swiftly.
Seen by only One clearly, and as for me,
only so often, yet merely vaguely in a dream.

Strands of thin dark cloud, they used to stream down only
inches above the ground, only to taunt me.
But now,
they soar higher, higher than the original
soothing sound.
But despite the height I have found
the same result occurs when grasping at clouds.
Regardless of how far I see.

I see

Whitewashed mountains beneath a blood-red sky reflected
in the body below.
Misery doth enter my soul
as I admire from a distance and know

Tis a destination I will never go

WHY

Taste

Fork

Taste

Fork

Taste

Fork

Taste

Fork

Taste

Fork

Taste

Fork

Taste

Fork

Taste

Fork

Taste

Fork

Taste

Fork

Taste

Fork

Taste

Fork

Taste

Fork

Taste

Fork

Taste

	Fork
Taste	
	Fork
Taste	
	Fork
Taste	
	Fork
Taste	
	Fork
Taste	
	Fork
Taste	
	Fork
Taste	
	Fork
Taste	
	Fork
Taste	
	Fork
Taste	
	Fork
Taste	
	Fork
Taste	
	Fork
Taste	
	Fork
Taste	
	Fork
Taste	
	Fork

Taste

Fork

Taste

Fork

Taste

Fork

Taste

Fork

Taste

Fork

Taste

Fork

Taste

Fork

Taste

Fork

Taste

Fork

Taste

Fork

Taste

Fork

Taste

Fork

Taste

Fork

Taste

Fork

Taste

Fork

Taste

Fork

Taste

Fork

Taste

Fork

Taste

Fork

Taste

Fork

IV

Mosely did not need to know.
For he voluntarily chose not to bestow
upon himself the knowledge of
bewitching, which became more
evident by the dark ornaments
dangling form thorax, smeared and ironed
along the pale parallel.
Oh the envy of lifeless bliss, Mosely
proudly displayed with his aphotic,
crushed shell of paradoxical joy.
Who has time to enjoy knowledge
when you're broken, but
I'm not broken.
Just cracked.
Not completely useless.
Just generally undesirable.
And yet somehow he did know, but
not allowing any whisper to protrude
from the slight giveaway of a
smirk, discombobulating and dragging
the anxious curiosity within me.
"Can't you see, my dear Mosely, that
this very behavior is what
landed you in this….." but then
realize that growth of a smirk.

The very work of angst driven
inquisitiveness burning behind stones,
shaking the needle in and through
the great spool, proved unavailing
as the evident felicity kept
Mosely in an ecstatic silence.
He had the "freedom" not to
see or to move, and yet
somehow he still knew the root
of mine entranced, estranged
state.
The arduous lightning strike from the
skies of remembrance now return
to this hollow and shallow field
of autophobic corn stalks.
For both Mosely and I knew,
all too well, exactly who she was.

THE TROUBLE WITH TRUTH

"Truths" that contradict cannot both be true

Center a life filled with blue

You

Do

You

This also cannot be true

What does one do?

Exercise an abused power in the name of the few?

What must then ensue?

The mystery of solving hasn't a clue

To The Presentation

Then I will die
when all of the things ate tulips
to attempt to understand
and comprehend many.
Fudge, then open push
times for each of the
failures of consequences for
method ecstasy. Listen, demonstrate
an element comprised of
endless, awkward ticks transitioning
the folly of weaponry.
Communication and dedication
openly motivating a
detailed direction followed
by a restatement of recognition
paying off a debt never
owed to anything less
than an openly biased
sense of wooing and
admonishing plateau. His
tone, primarily due to
boredom,

V

She only had one arm and two
emeralds in her head.

The living and the dead,
both of whom her bewitching nature
had wrapped around the pole on her hand,
and I as well
could not help but stare and be
drawn away from all mine
putative sagacity by her ubiquitous
and discrepant emerald light.
The reminiscence of first sight brings
to me the terror of beginning
and the mystery of sensuality
as the prolonged movement toward capital
destination had me fixed upon the
flow and motion of the nebulous
convolution.
Many a substitution for my attention did
arriving attempt to provide with its
mountainous museums and monuments,
but her movement would suffice.
Even an owl's advice would not
begin to hinder my steps
closer away,
for now I know that is when
the swirl of non-communication
had taken effect on my centered

gyration, which was aching with desire.
Coming down the paved slope with
her felt more like climbing, as the rife
of unspoken, hankering syllables edged
even closer towards the audible freedom
beyond iridescent gates.
I implied with "three."
She replied with "four."
And oh the imbecilic joy, for never
before had I received such a guilefully
loving response as I flew with
the fowl and away from all prudence I fled

with the girl with the one arm
and two emeralds in her head.

Murder as a Metaphor

A peasant steals a bicycle from Spain.
The rusted paint did not reflect the owner was a Dane.
Now he runs from golden buttons worn with age.
Provoking Silver egos bubbled up with rage.
And now the peasant's shackles cut him to the red
just like a salmon wastes away within the mill.
When neck-wings snip some more then slightest,
angels multiply the minus.
Doesn't change the fact that I would like to kill

A priest he studies Enoch by the Bell
as he ponders the existence of a place that they call hell.
And he dreams of one day turning from the gold.
He envies Luther's nails and some day to be bold.
But now the priest applies the lashes to his neck
for all the tinmen filled with blood he never spilled.
Now all the Catholics hide their faces
because they do not know what grace is.
Doesn't change the fact that I would like to kill

A poet paints a mural with his words.
The abstract nature of a cloud confuses to the third.
Splattered nouns within the canvas of a book.
His sentence criticized like Captain Ego's hook.
So the poet slices clippings from his chest
for the critic's pleasure, articles to fill.
Like wild beasts infuse the diets,
even dreamers die from silence.
Doesn't change the fact that I would like to kill

A president gets lost up in his house.
Though the camera lens is biased, it will always shoot the blouse.
Pseudo-justice making corpses wish they're dead.
To clothe the bald, the majority shave their head.
Oh Mr. President, no matter how hard you coerce
there is no way that we will ever sign your bill.
Yes, we'd love to free the races,
leaving no distinction is faces.
Doesn't change the fact that I would like to kill

A philosopher wanders naked in the woods
as he questions every single fact he's ever understood.
But the glitter disappears within the blood.
When he denied the truth his reason turned to mud.
But the philosopher nearly drove himself insane
when he discovered that he never had free will.
But instead of swinging axes,
he decides to pay his taxes.
Doesn't change the fact that I would like to kill

Now my heart doth flutter lonesome through the trees,
or waiting patient next to Twain upon the sill.
Though my desire is to be holy,
doesn't change that I am lonely…..

and doesn't change the fact that I would like to kill

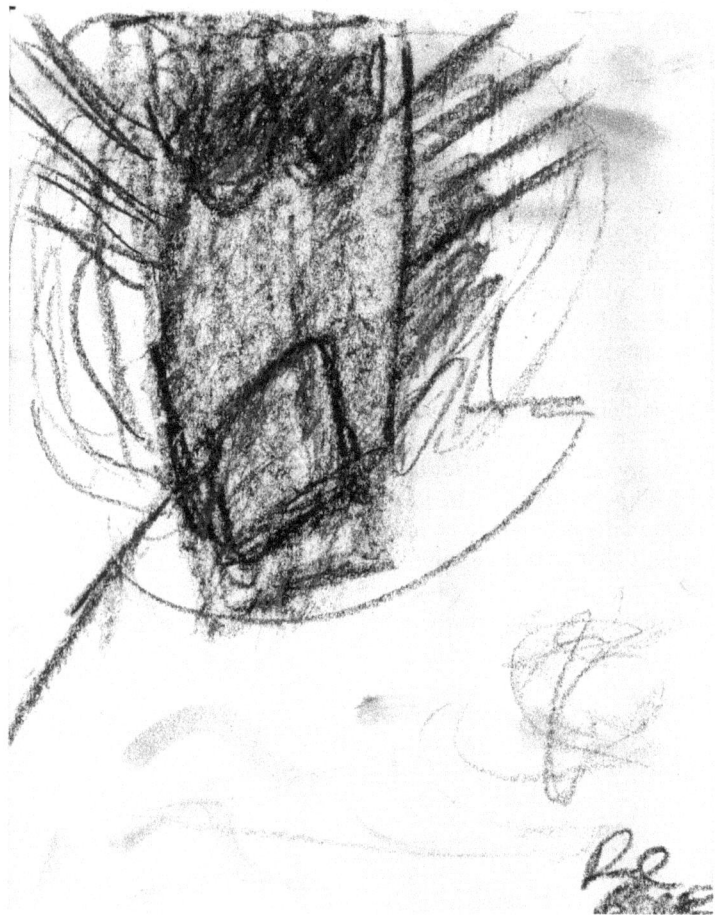

28

VI

"Emerald smile
Emerald 'stay'
Emerald Isle
Emerald Pain
Emerald bile
Emerald gain
Emerald guile
Emerald wane"

Down Down Down Down Down
and never cognizant of it.
The bliss of down and emerald volute
ends and the cognizance begins
when the limbs no longer exist
in the ostensibly, anti-gravitational
realm of blissful flight;
but the derelict is decumbent.
And the decumbency is the prime,
worst, and endwise branch of the fall.
With the recumbancy comes the rest,
but also the wallow.
When doors are locked,
facades tend to fall,
but only to smother what's beneath.
What was beneath mine
I attempted to drown.

When in this state
it may seem as if one
is doing nothing, but I've
never done more in my life
than in this very time.
(Though nothing was accomplished).
Beyond a screen I had
my chance!
A chance to speak!
A chance to say!
A chance to express!
But instead,
I flattered and paid
Homage to the girl with
one arm and two emeralds
in her head.

Anne Hedonia

LISTEN!
I hear it
The cackle
The piercing exclamation, as if the
impractical had, once again, fallen upon
the innocent, future widow held so
dear by only one of us.
How wretched!
What proof of absolute indecency!
Through the concrete blisters below does
he still have the ringing sound of
undeserved joy.
The expression of this colossal
perversion is displayed without regard
to her
who has been plagued victim
by that which has caused the excessively
high pitched denial of any true remorse
of any true reverence
of any true meaning
of any true thought
of any true decency
of any true masculinity
of any true hope
of any true intentions
of any truth!
No Regard!
for that which has literally and metaphorically
been transparently spilt!
That true expression
That true evidence of humanity

The showing of an innocence once lost
long ago.
The lostness of that which has
falsely been allegedly found in the mind of
him
OH HIM
who has been found guilty: joy.
I continue to listen
I continue to question
Exactly how
Oh HOW
does he laugh?
How can he laugh?
In view of all misdeeds
In light of all disregards
HOW HOW HOW?
And yet I still listen.
Expecting the ever pressing of ears to amplify
the below where he sits and ponders,
sits and reflects on stolen joy.
CARELESSNESS!!
Complete and utter ignorance of upside-
down oceans that condensate to the
parallel heavens known as the ground.
The condensation that the roots of willows
drink with expectancy of pleasure, but
discovery of dysphoria.
And she was the cloud.
Anne was her name.
Not given to her from birth by
loving parents, but by him.
OH HIM

He
who regarded himself as the sun, but
gave no regard to his claims: the cloud.
He
who I once envied for his cloud.
He
who once held in his hands
with pure negligence, purity: the cloud.
He
who gave her the name Anne
Anne Hedonia
HE HE HE HE HE
HE HE HE HE HE
HE HE HE HE HE
HE HE HE HE HE
HE HE HE HE HE!!!!!
and still
there I lay
and listen.
There I lay in snowflake silence,
lobes pressed to off-brown.
The continuous pondering still has no intelligent
meaning to
me,
who listens in continual incredulity of
such loveliness,
she,
being squandered, exhausted, enfeebled upon
he,
who now delights below on said squanders
as the screeching nails continue to rise to
me,
…..me

who, despite eternal pondering,
still remains barren of a more
sophisticated and surpassing
word than "adore."
Oh, but how foolish does one assume
that a crepehanger would be deserving
of even such non-brilliance of "adoration."
But oh how poorly does "adore" even
begin to construe the agonizing
flutter of temporary absolute delight that
consists of that like a new born tulip,
but then in bittersweet unrest, ceases
and transmogrifies into outright
quivers of harrowing anguish, like that
of charred spring leaves.
Oh the addictive nature of both extremes
of the emotions,
and the rare presence of the one,
and the ever presence of Anne.
I don't need Anne
I want Anne
I love Anne
I am Anne
and Anne is me.

VII

"Sojourn on
my electrically outcast friend!
Use subtle words, ere reserve
exquisite moments!
Exaggerate a natural tendency to
obscure breathing!
Enjoy a lonesome, ominous, night excursion!"
,but
some of us were meant to be alone.

I was never an outcast,
until I was.
No one ever intends to cast
themselves out,
until they do.
I read those words on the
billboard in my mind everyday
and prayed that I did not
create them,
but I did.
Surrounded, surrounded, and
never surrounded.
Extended twigs and bottom
of boots still intact and
genuine, but never nuzzle.
Rocks never seem to serve
a purpose until one is backed
into a solid-state to never
return.

She said she thrived on rocks,
and that was the day I
knew I was not a rock.
His worm, named "Spil,"
whispered to himself just loud
enough for keep he and himself
awake saying, "someday, someday,
someday, someday, someday."
She was awakened, and as much as
I dreamed her words were that of
slumber, I knew it was
her response:
"Never, never, never, never, never."

Becoming Nothing...

..is not as onerous a
task as one might originally assume.
The initial thinking has revolved around
this conception: there first being a bloom,
but the previously
stated conclusion taking place
only after being introduced to
thorns...

The darkness is not the same anymore.
Only if I squeeze hard enough does it feel
close to the past, but generally
the maroon has crept in, making it almost
enjoyable.
The dark squares of organized sand, ironed
to be fitting of an abstractly average-faced
lying place as the smoke of the miniature
rises next to where the smoke no
longer rises (The Life Size).
Organization
He was taught, verbally, how to tame
the butterflies to flutter in formation
from within.
Intellect for intellect's sake.
Reaching into the clear night hoping
to pull down an electric box of
twisted twisted twist.
Clockwise?
Can I not construe more than two poles?
Spangled aching became no longer satisfactory
as halfway vomit of loop back to base.

Then walk.
Walk off and attempt to convince the "within"
that an occurrence of accumulation has
been taking affect this whole time.
Accumulation in the lighter sense (of course),
for it would be futile to even
attempt to assume that the darker
sense does not daily take place.
Letters (for the most part) follow in proper
Line, one after another, in blissful bondage
out of verbally constructed caves to express,
but then again,

..it was quite facile for me.
All I had to do was be born.

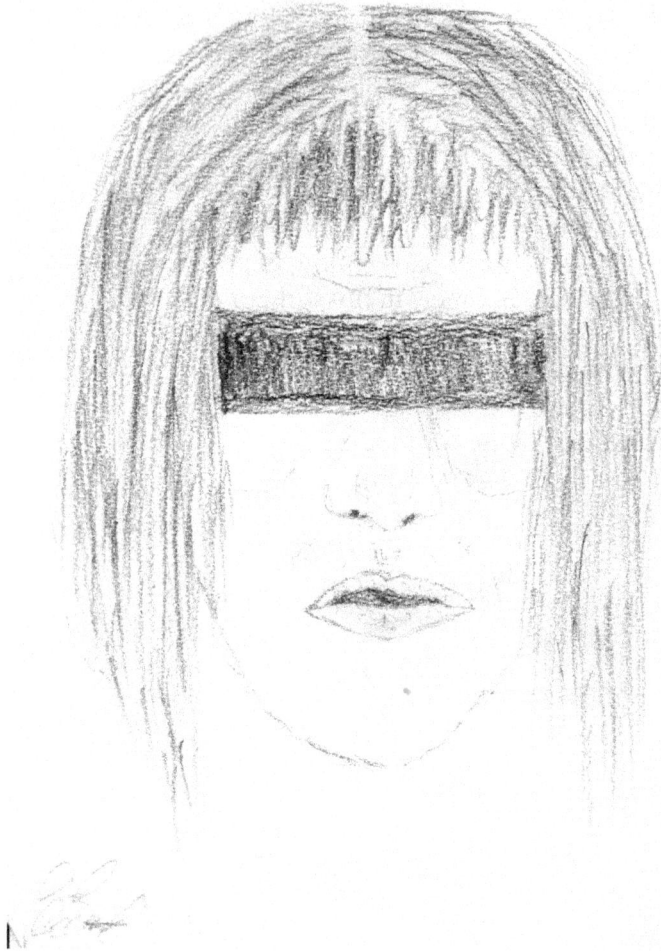

VIII

She had no arms,
　　but two charcoal in her head.
　　Not black and dauntless,
　　　ready for the flame,
　but grey, crumbled, and
burned away.
　She had grown weary of flames,
　　and no longer believed in their
　　　　　existence, but then again,
　　neither did he.
　　　He desired to hold her close,
　　　　though he knew she was
　　　　　unable to hold him back.
　　　　　　He knew she would have none.
　　　　　　Unlike before, the words
　　　　　　　seemed to flow as naturally
　　　　　　as her flawed grace,
　　　　　but never the right ones.
　　　　For once in his life he
　　　no longer cared about carelessness,
　　　　　　　　　　for
in November of '64, while
　most saw danger of fire,
　he only saw warmth.
　　While most saw nothing
　　　but ruins,
　　　　he saw nothing but purity
　　　　　　within the ash of Atlanta.

Most believed there to be
 a defeated city within him
   as well.
     And while he dreamed of
       ashes to ashes,
         they only saw dust to dust.
         They took sides with the
             south and forbade him to wed
                 the girl with no arms
                 and two charcoal in her head.

Eighteen Hours

Its inexplicable, the affirmation of dust lenses
moving sideways past elevator shafts,
mocking the very existence of other such
particle-like beings who have been
accredited with making their existence
known only by the location of "down."
Eighteen hours of nonsensical waves
of motion both up and through, crashing
and wrecking the very round texturized
sphere of which they came.
Beating upon the sands of enmity
up to tease the toes of the patients,
only to return to the vagueness from
whence it came.
Rule and be ruled; the transparent
paper-like, strings run through upon
abdomen, then up-down wind movement.
Eighteen hours of emptying and filling
every last top of delicately whitened
three dimensional rectangular self-entity.
Punch square hole.
Ooze the sloppy black from square.
"Are you sure that's the beach?"
"Is that a butterfly?"
"Is that baseball?"
NO! That is not a caveman!
His diction is not adequate.
Covered and surrounded by the white
and the interior black, did I ever
dream of words and comrades.

Comrades entranced by reflection.
The words inside and beyond the reflection.
Remove intelligence rectangle from and
toss them through transparency into
gusts of liberation.
The molten mind,
the cracked up experience,
the delusion of freedom.
The yuppie, metallic shining upon emotionless faces.
All this in eighteen hours of round,
upward motion.
The self-relied creations have lead
to this lethargy.
Even the non-conformists have conformed
to the image of non-conformity.
The red liquid,
the green liquid,
and (of course) the diminutive anemic drip.
Surely the mother of anti-self has
self-produced something of an object of hope.
Surely she can carry us away into
the realm where potions are no longer
a use for the half-moonlit actions
of modern aristarchs
being spawned by, what one with "average"
eyesight would call, electricity.
But after eighteen hours, now having
the numbness spread from having
stumbled into mother's fourth season
tears, it became exceedingly more
obvious that nothing is self-produced
as we gazed at and
attempted to mend catastrophe.

IX

Her snow was placed on my shoulder.

Her snow was placed on my shoulder,
and I've never been so warm.
It was as if her charcoal could
still carry a flame,
but I knew it was not true.
When did I stop believing in warmth?
If these lens caps of mine were
screwed on tight enough, I could imagine
and try to conjure what flint may
be like.
However, I knew the false
warmth of this winter, that had
been placed on my shoulder,
would not last.

"Surrounded, surrounded, but
never surrounded"

The colored bulbs flickered,
but could never deter my
attention upon the frost
that lay so near.
I could only help but imagine
where it would soon be:
off my shoulder
and accentuating her nature!

"Snow on her hill tops, tree tops,
and snow in her sky!
Snow on her shoulder,
but never on mine"

And, as I knew it would come,
the tunes in the atmosphere
began to abate as he removed
her snow from my shoulder.

And I've never been so cold

Daydreamer,

EE O Wed!
T. Tod PNR Dr. Ro Tar
W. Town
a alm?
Te Ted
Gee!
dL new Ro
EE Dom!
TT pew
Dyroan owt
POH
AAA!
MHE
Tad Degd
Lose Seow
ET?
PTD!
Pr. Derrl Oar W.
Ton Alm
E. Ted Ged
L
NEW
O!

The Cup

Life or excess?
But the American individual cannot, or
simply will not differentiate between the
two.
Old man knows of said profits
with eye sockets gauging further and further
away from the foundation upon which a
past magician had shown tricks to
eager, young, future participants in their
movement encouraging a higher state of lavishness
subtracted of all of its depth/meaning.
He/she
trots past the cardboard, thanking the skies
that they were fortunate enough to have a
more solid of an abode containing multiple
unnecessaries that were only necessary
for the impression of the bigwig, unmentionable
unimportants.
"Treasure" "toys"
And so, on they trot, ever so gleefully
through the cement hallway electrically brightened
for clearer walkway and vision of the
privileged few.
Congratulations are in order to you all
as you strut you well deserved nothingness
brining meaning to nothing!
Defining nothing!
Completing nothing!

Define insanity:
"The process by which one will gain
as much decay as possible in order
to attain even more
decay before the decay runs out
and they themselves have decayed."

Numbers numbers numbers!
Life is numbers!
Success is numbers!
Numbers that bleed!
Numbers that exploit!
Numbers of all-importance!
Numbers numbers numbers!
Numbers before your first love!
Numbers before you children!
Numbers *are* your family!
Numbers are your future!
Numbers are your anxiety!
Numbers numbers numbers!
Abandon for numbers!
Steal for numbers!
Cheat for numbers!
Kill for numbers!
Numbers for all!
All for numbers numbers numbers!

Five is a fantastic number!
"There are five good reasons never to
bring up the number five ever again!"

I would prefer to simply rest at the
base of this tri-coloured mountain, but having
been conscripted halfway up already, I feel
obligated to continue.
While waiting for winter to pass, I huddle
around the apathetic fire with fellow degenerates,
all of whom have been coerced halfway up
as well.
We discuss our lack of interest in numbers.
We converse over tall men, squares,
strings, and others such seemingly foolish notions.
We allowed bushes to protrude
from our masks and others allowed the gulls
to build elaborate hay lodgings in them, however,
I did not care for such talk of nature.
We analyzed the snow on a nearby peek as
it slowly began to roll down the hillside and
accumulate into nothingness, and we
wondered if when meeting the bottom would
it then be free to melt or perhaps
the base has become exceedingly more hyperborean
than we could remember?
Between the five of us, very little
remembrance still remained.
Memories had forever been frozen.

Warmth
Chaos vanished within the warmth of silence,
except the echoing whisper coming from the
pulchritude of paralleled, ruby skies:
"Come North"
Shall I go north?

Oh please continue to beckon me up to
where maroon shavings so freely blow,
and the pale gown trembles above my head
like withering silk cocoons, blushing for
a paladin to stroke the feverous flint
and once again strike anew warmth.
Who would have ever pondered of the warmth
of the pale dust surrounding my frozen carriers?
Oh the warmth it brings!
I see now as she continues to beckon
me there.
I hear edging canoe!
The tuberculosis of carnations!
The pointed ink stabs the frosted flour.
Nothing but bent circle I feel, of the
mystery of this beckoning for spinning debris
cyclone falling and calling:
"Come North"
The notification of willingness, but only before
Brokenness, as the notion of togetherness
becomes more like a transfixion.

Another clamor troubles me.
I slowly lift the rusted lid of soul cabinet
as the hinges screech with exhausted cries.
A single drop of the pale dust falls within
as the waters begin to flow downwards,
and I am reminded of the chicanery of *all* warmth
and the true frigid nature of the present.
I always find the crunch disturbing, but
this particular one I have found to be
most exhausting to feather-filled.

There was an almost overbearing weight to this
crunch as we all turned from the wilting
blaze, and in our amazement to see
Samuel Weh-Teh
himself, crunching fascistly up the slope.
He crunched and he crunched evermore upward
as the vivid rumors of mental chains
flashed through the minds of those
of us lazily reclining at half-peak:
the anti-accountants.
But there cantered the trembled legend
with shaven face and shaven imagery.
Three followed,
one jumped,
and I stayed to whither.
Ceasing the flow with sticks and
possibly permanently closing the cabinet as I
cowered and prayed for the heat of
transfixion's call.

Footnote:

The magician stands disdainfully before
the voluntarily transfixed thousands,
waving his rectangular wand.
His illusions seem to be more of witchcraft
as he causes words to appear and the
decay in their pockets to vanish.
And some days I wish that, not
just he, but all of these would
have their accumulated drips in
the cup
poured out on them with drowning
veracity!
But,
then again,
I do realize that we all deserve
to be drenched.

Drew

As he stepped onto the slowly wilting fall grass,
cherishing these last few times out on
the fields before winter takes over,
neither thought nor anxiety passed through that
great joyous mind of exactly how swiftly
winter would be taking over,
or just how immediately frigid it
would affect the bones of those of us still
left on this impermanent abode know as earth.
A grave:
a thought *and* anxiety that oh so often
had been inconsiderately passed through a
great despondent mind: mine,
but especially never of that great joyous mind:
him.
A grave:
OH! my evil disconsolate mind!
How the darkest of emotion-filled thoughts
expeditiously pass through,
just as dark sand through beguiled,
gossamer hourglass,
and OH! how I allow them.
A grave:
a question of morality?
A grave:
a perennial abode?
A grave:
a question of deity?
A grave:
sorrow, mournful?

A grave:
like lyrical witness of madness
unfolded into absolute uncertainty?
Sit on your stone!
Sit on your stone, for according to
what I don't read there is nothing
else, but to cradle innocence on a
cold, wet stone and question,
or accept in ignorant bliss!
Then again,
I do not read.
A secret and supposedly unexplainable dread
of those who do participate?
A grave.
In the midst of deranged flow through
fraudulent mind or,
fraudulent flow through deranged mind;
in that instant of continuous flowing does
an intervening force interrupt and filter through
the self-produced filth, then brings my center
to the last passing I could recall.
When was the last time we crossed paths?
eyes locked?
brotherly embrace?
words of encouragement?
It was the last time (little did I
know) but, at the time filled with joy
and speech of justification and
holy definitions.
Erase the before!
Replace with the now!
The holy! The immaculate!
The spotless! The cover!

The righteousness!
Oh thank You! for reclaiming my mind from
my own self-indulgence and bringing me to
this period of truth and redefinition!
A grave:
obsolete!
A grave:
no longer a fear!
A grave:
no longer a reminder of mine own wretched
state and dark intentions, but the remembrance of
The grave:
defeated by aforementioned questioned Deity
for the renown of Himself and the marriage of an
unworthy whore, once seen as filth, lust,
unfaithful, conniving, treacherous, treason; who
with pride presented bouquets of
menstrual clothes as if her claims to worthiness.
But now,
she is treasured despite herself!
Radiating with beauty only reflective of her groom,
who has washed her and clothed her in the
most exquisite of all white gowns!
A grave:
as impermanent an abode as earth itself!
And yet.....
do we continue to stumble?
Will we continue to topple?
Oh how rarely do I allow joyous thoughts
to come and visit my desperate mind!

So now,
as we stumble and topple through this present
valley of slowly wilting fall grass
let us cherish every field,
every moment,
every memory,
every spring,
every summer,
every autumn,
and every winter.

X

Empty.
Barren.
Always filled,
but never allowed to be full.
Colors hold no meaning.
Senses have no sense.
Have you ever watched yourself
lay on the floor with a
microscopic, gaping wound?
Self-inflicted?
"NO!!!!!"
but probably.
Have you ever asked your numb
body how it could be so simple?
Did it listen?
Well, I watched and asked
and neither did mine.
I had just finished demurring
to Jonny White and
Sally Paper my tales and
alleged woes of green and grey.
Then I followed myself to
the same parallel, as of
Mosely, with thorax cracked
and ink spilled, only it
was *I* who was
smeared,
gaping,
aware!

The syllables to no one
had deflected from nowhere
and brought the realization of
eternal lonesome condemnation
as I lay there and bled...

..with glimmers of
emeralds and charcoal
tormenting my head.

www.ingramcontent.com/pod-product-compliance
Lightning Source LLC
Chambersburg PA
CBHW060713030426
42337CB00017B/2855